VOICES & VENUES In VERSE!

The Gathering

By -
KENNETH J. HESTERBERG

ISBN 978-1-62806-318-9

Library of Congress Control Number 2021907770

Published by Salt Water Media
29 Broad Street, Suite 104
Berlin, MD 21811
www.saltwatermedia.com

Cover photo, courtesy of:
P/Lt Larry G. Davies; Cambridge Sail and Power Squadron

Primary Editor: Janet Jones

The Gathering of "it"

Separate things of "like",
Seek alliances of a kind,
For comfort, opportunity, protection,
And, many other reasons defined!

Humans apply the names,
To classify and categorize things:
Animals in Herds__ or other as
Lions in Prides, Canines in packs;
Fish in schools; Birds in Flocks;
Bees in Hives; Harvests in Markets;
Humans in Neighborhoods; classes;
Organizations; Congregations; Unions;
Leagues; Armies; Parties; Troops__
And, many others, somewhat the same,
Combinations that, coalesce into
Groupings of convenience together!
A "Gathering of Reason!"

This "Gathering" is the coming together,
Of diverse short stories in verse,
Of bits and pieces, this and that,
Items of interest, items of fact,
Some of levity, others a serious bent,
But all, spark an interest to have,
To, catch your eye, mind & thought.
To enjoy and to be reread, throughout life!

Maybe, to cause you, a pen to find,
And scribe your own stories in verse
Or prose__ as a legacy for your heirs!
For, if not, those tales, be lost in time!

Dedication

To the Nelson Weller Sr. "Clan"
From whence my "bride" came,
And, all those so associated,
Thru, birth and marriage!

I dedicate this book!

No names
Do I list,
For to
Miss one
Would be
Unfair, and a slight!

But, to the clan, like family mine!
Prize I__ each member, & each branch!
For knowing it or not,
They have added to the books I have penned!
To the generations then, now & to find,
My best wishes are tendered.

This "Gathering" of words in verse
A literary endeavor of a type!
Touching on aspects of life
And, living in places to find.
There are subjects of interest_
That, are readily found,
To challenge one's mind
And others, of pure enjoyment,
Hopefully a delight, to come upon!

Table of Contents

Books by KJH in the series: VOICES & VENUES IN VERSE!

The World of Water
Fair winds and foul, beacons, lighthouses, on ocean, rivers & bays, or in the deep!
Yesterdays, Other Days and Holidays
Holidays of humankind, Tributes, Recognitions & Remembrances!
Inspiration
Thoughts the additive, for the engine of humankind!
Inspiration Two & too!
Self-motivation through life!
Moments in Time and Scope!
Memories, ideas, capacity for achievement, vastness for self!
Of People and Spaces!
Space like most things in life, only a restriction of the human self!
Choices, Chances & Life!
Choices- to make! Chances_ one takes! Life_ a gift of worth!
VISTAS!
Visions of the beholder, seen, felt & sensed, memory markers!
"Tapestry" of Life Spun!
Woven through ones life, how good when done, depends on the path chosen!
"Earth Tones!"
Majestic in color & sound, there, where ere you go_ your gift!
"Earth Rhythms!"
Earth's rhythms playing on this planet's scene, there to grab and hold!
"Rebound"
A skill to perfect, to better your life!
"Baker's Dozen!"
When a dozen becomes 13, short stories in Verse, touching heart, soul and mind!
"XIV"
A tribute to days when numbers, were letters, and no zeros could be found!
"The Gathering:"
Of, a like group, human and none human, together find a kindred ship!

Written and awaiting publication!
"Intuition!"
Perhaps a touch of magic, or ESP, or remnants found in one's DNA!
"Turns"
Actions that influence the direction of life!
"Mélange"
"This, that and the other", to capture your invested moments!
"Diversity"
Life's colors, sounds, feelings and times!

All cover photos are waters near the Chesapeake Bay_
my muse since childhood.

The verses "Short Stories" meant to be read, throughout life!

Prologue

This is the fifteenth book,
In the series of: "Voice and Venues in Verse".
And in the other books,
A title was in mind, and the verses,
Written, to that target!

Not so this time,
I went through a long period of writing,
Where, subjects, & words, kept coming!
And I was well nearing,
The number of words to draft a book,
And still not a definitive title!

Then a phone call, from a relative,
Inviting me to a get-together,
At a "Gathering" to include a large number,
From one side of the family!
And, the name for this book
Was born and quite appropriate!

The opportunity exists,
For you good reader, to join,
A "Gathering" of diverse short stories in verse,
Throughout the pages, of this book__
An exploration of a kind,
Of subject matter, available, to enjoy now__
And to reread, throughout your life!

I hope "The Gathering" serves you well!

π

Gathering of the Bloodline

In the two sides of family mine,
I remember not, ever__
Full, family reunions!
Why not, I cannot say,
But, were foreign, as country gone!

We would see folks,
On visits, at times now and then,
But never in large groups__
Just for meeting, eating and fun!
And, it wasn't until later in life,
The question, begged me, to ask: why not?

With my wife's family, the story different,
And because I was married within,
Reunions, not yearly, but often
Was a fact, and if faces seen__
On a street or elsewhere,
Recognized you, as part of the kin!

But as the years flowed by,
And some grew old and even died,
The coming generations,
Got lost in the changing, tide!

And even I, as an in-law,
Rued the fact, that those days__
Of "The Gatherings" were lost!

In todays chaotic world,
Relatives live far and wide,
And somehow, for reason un-clear,
Family, is too soon__ put aside!
And now, I recognize, a chance missed,
To have helped __ a "Gathering," to be supplied!

But perhaps,
That the verse I pen,
In short stories diverse,
Are, as my children and relatives
And when compiled into titled books,
Is and are **"The Gathering"**
Of my life now, and I invite you to attend!

π

A Fish Fantasy

Suppose, just suppose,
Like a shark your life would be!
And, all throughout your living time,
Each moment for you__ movement was your need!

How long do you think you would survive?
And, how long do you think,
You would want to abide__
If in motion you were all the time?

I, don't know__ so don't ask me!
But, I bet-you__
One tired "so-in-so", would be!

Tis no wonder,
Sharks are teed-off, at everything in the sea!
Or is that not the reason__
Could it be, their shark skin "suit"___
Just doesn't suit__ for afternoon tea?

Just a thought in humor, to entertain!

π

Bridges of Time

The winds did blow,
And, bent the leafless limbs
And put the clinging snow to flight!
Just short days to the Equinox,
And, from its bitter days,
At the ides of March,
Mother Nature sent, one last,
Winter blast to bite!

Behind the blow,
Poised to batter house and hill,
Was, this final onslaught
Of icy cold__ to warrant,
Heavy coat and scarf,
And chilled bones,
On our trip to Sunday Service!

True "spring" now just days in the offing!
The winter, long and hard
And, I never thought to say,
But, good it be__
To put sled and snow shovel away!

Even the mud and mire,
Of melt and April rains,
Honed a warm spot in my heart,
This year, a winter to remember__
And dread, when the next is to start!

How well I remember 1939__
Of my, High School Graduation
And, my enlistment in the
Flying Tigers,
Not many will remember,
The Tigers now!

Me, most likely one of the last,
And, one, of those,
To come, out of WWII
To a different world,
A different time!

Now my 100th birthday passed,
A century gone__ Good God!
And me, the family Patriarch__
Good, Grief!
Perhaps, the black sheep made good!
I let out a chuckle!

My family, a good bunch__
And, in my way, I love them all!
I guess, especially,
That great, great granddaughter,
She's got spunk!

She's nestled, now in my arm,
And leans close and whispers,
I love you gramps!
And, my words are:
"Back at you, my last love!"

- - - - -

"Words garnered, from one,
Of that greatest generation__
Then, woven together
*To honor all, and embarrass none_*
To each and all of that group,
"Well done, and gratitude lasting"!

Soon now, the last of them to be____ gone!

π

Generational Change

There was a time,
In days gone by,
When my generation knew,
That the world was different then,

Of course you and I,
My "old friend" then__
Had ages near the same,
As a new decade did begin!

We lived the time,
Near the end, of a depression great,
Followed by a war,
Even worse than the one before!

And then, those,
Followed in Korea, by a "police action",
That, was politically named__
Now, has lasted, half century more!

And, even more conflict in the world,
At places and spaces,
Where, few Americans,
Had spent their blood, before!

Then another century,
A new millennium came,
Printed its number,
On calendars to be seen!

And those of my father's generation,
We, and they noted,
There were, blanks in their ranks,
Where, soon, none would be seen!

But, for some the world was a better place,
For others little changed! Then in the USA____
Death and destruction on 9-11 came,
Innocents lost; hero's made, little solved!

Yes, the tale had been spun,
When from the swamp, humans had come!
And readapted, unnumbered times before!
And, seemed, would forever more!

Tis a shame you surely can see__
That, humans with races estranged,
Have not, the will nor the brains,
To take advantage of life's opportunity!

So a query I put to all,
How much longer can humans,
Be permitted, on Earth to abide?
When their stupidity__ they cannot hide!

Now that my generation,
Is being left behind, as many die!
And, there are others, already in line,
Will none of these__ change the tide?

And, bring races, creeds and religions,
Together in brotherhood,
Or, should the world, just take a pill__
And end earth__ of its ills?

Today as the Earth gets worse,
With weather and decline,
There may not be a better time__
For humankind to change, that tide!

To repair Earth, and humankind!
Why not now, say I?

Maybe COVID 19__ in this day and time;
Will educated the peoples of the world
How, too better life for al!
It could be done__
For "kin" under the skin__ are we all!

π

News

The Daffodils know winter is done!
And, it's not yet spring!
Will snow come,
And knock those flowers down?

Will there be snow,
Before the seasonal Equinox__
Comes without a roaring sound?

Or, is this year and Climate Change,
Playing a deadly deceptive game?
You know, questions like this,
Make one wonder,
About, Global Warming!

All this,
With a little common sense__
Even the dumbest human being,
Can realize, "Mother Nature"
Has been unhappy for quite a while!

So, the question is; is it too late__
Too placate Mother Nature?

Let's hope Mother__ her children will forgive,
And, give humankind, another chance, yet to live!
π

Only Seldom, Return

I find it somewhat natural,
When you return to a "place",
After time elapses,
A comparison you make,
Of the present visit,
And, one or more you made before!

Right, wrong, or in between
One feels the anxiety,
Fostered by, the changes spliced in!
Usually, memory, wants the old__
To remain or return!
There is comfort, in what was known!

But, when the doing is done,
The chance of return,
Anytime soon, usually__
Not worth the wait begun!
Only in time, maybe, it is partially spun!

The thing I found for me to do,
And this might be good advice for you,
Is to capture all you can in memories,
And, when tis time for change,
Hold those memories tightly.
Knowing they're at your beck and call!

Then, buy into the changes of the day,
For it, may not be as bad as you think!
If it is__ that old memory will see you, through!
And maybe, two memories will be better than one!

From the old-timer's "Handbook of Frustration"

π

On The Road

I was never a tourist—type!
Just give me a canoe, or boat,
Or, a pair, of good hiking boots__
And more than, happy would be!

But, now in my more mature years__
As I tune in the "TV" travel shows,
Reluctantly admit,
I missed more than "one boat!"

I missed much in learning,
Of those Ancestors,
Who, shared, their DNA, with me,
From places abided, far and wide!

Those, many things__
Like architecture, art, music,
Sports, gastronomic adventures,
And lands, of worth, to see!

Many there were, of human accomplishments__
With muscle, insight and determination,
Back when, with little mechanization__
Brought magnificent structures, to see!

And, those great, civilizations,
With large populations__
Larger than first understood,
Were there, many millennia ago!

Demise, by war, bias, greed, nature,
Have cheated humanity,
Of noting, all undertaken,
By those ancestors, we never knew!
They made haste in their time,

And with what was known and learned,
Made a world better to view!
But, what seems fatalistic of humankind＿

With every two steps forward,
Time soon, took a step back,
And unfortunately,
That still is the fate of today!

Look back in time,
The fall into the dark ages,
And the hundreds of years,
Before the renaissances' did arrive!

And on back, and then forward＿ we go,
Tis wise to know history well,
For as the saying goes,
When you learn not from history,
Repetition is to be, the game played!

History does portend＿ the future!
Unfortunately, tis the path laid＿
That humankind, neglects, to change,
Maybe, just＿ maybe, one day will,
Who knows?

π

Epilogue: And the situation, will not be solved,
Until each of us, realize we are the solution!
How to bring this thought to the fore?
Just maybe COVID 19, this has done.
Only, time will tell!

π

From on High

Listen oh listen,
Yea children of Earth!
Some words of wisdom,
Hear me__ disburse!

Tis not, that you haven't,
Heard them before,
But, take to heart,
For never, did you explore!

But, urge you now__
Listen and action take,
For "time" is precious,
And, less and less,
Can humankind, forsake__
To change, direction!
A great deal is required__
If on Earth__ humans, are to retire!

The world is shaking to its core,
Global Warming
And, Climate Change
Warnings, louder than before!

Each day, you refuse to believe,
What urgings you see and hear,
Is, one less day__
That, humankind will be here!

If "man" continues his destructive ways,
Not even your bones, hidden in graves
Will be saved!
Gone will be all, except viruses and germs!

π

A Stage in Age

Smart was I, in times gone by__
But now my memory has deserted me.
I feel bad each day,
When words I cannot say,
But, constantly, they are teasing me!

And then, in the middle of the night,
I wake, with a word or a sight,
Lost in the beauty of the day!

Is the Lord, or is Satan,
Or both, telling me,
It's almost time__ to come their way!

This I know is a fact for sure,
For no one, gets out of life alive!
But, there are things,
I feel yet, I am to do!

Is this, just, a dream,
Or a nightmare,
I am living, through?

If I am able to arise in the dawn,
With, another day to carry on!
Perhaps, all will come clear.

And, I will know,
What, lies a head for me__
If not__ dead is dead!

But, then, know my calendar is clear__
When a call, from heaven or hell,
Will be, the voice I hear!

π

The Last Hurrah

In a time before "old" did come,
When that gang of ours',
With teen years, close to done__
Got together in an Easter Time!

And headed to Herald Harbor,
On the upper river Severn,
In Maryland, where all were from,
For a weekend of only guys
And, some "Stag" like fun!

Easter was late that year,
So spring was well underway,
Trees had green, and blossoms found.
And that summer cottage__
Became, our holy ground!

We all had pitched in,
For staples to buy,
So some of the guys,
Stopped, for food to bring,
Others, bottles of stuff to try!

And, my navigator, and I,
A case or more of beer
Was, our target, to obtain__
And, not get arrested__
For underage still the same!

I'll not name the place we stopped,
But most likely, not, there today!
And ready to leave, were we__
With the bill all paid__
When in walked the fuzz__ a cop!

Honestly I'll say,
I thought our big weekend was done,
But, he didn't pull his gun,
He winked at my buddy and me,
And, nodded us on our way!

This was a story to share with the gang,
And what a weekend for a memory had!
Playing cards, and enough or more to drink
and eat, and talking trash,
Before, all were sick mostly in the sink!

Oh yes, we learned first hand,
What, booze could do to a lesser man.
And, most ran for the windows or doors,
With heads stuck out,
As illness roared!

It wasn't funny then,
But now it seems__ so
Many bellies in "morning" emptied out__
On one poor slob,
Sleeping, on a cot, on a porch below!

After the laughter and tears,
And, clean-up was done!
To the beach we all went,
For, "a most refreshing swim"
Remember reader__ it was April early!

Me, in all the horsing around,
I cut the ball of my foot,
On an oyster shell,
And my blood flowed very proud,
And, still have that scar, as a reminder now!

Unfortunately, that was,
The beginning of the end,
There was college, the military,
And, work, moving and life to live__
And the songs, we sung, not sung again!

Many or most, of those guys,
Are now gone__ age does call the shots,
I know one is still around,
For he was my Best Man,
And, a year later I was his!

Come 2021, will be their 65th Anniversary,
And my bride will be gone 8 years__
And that weekend at the beach___
Is, already six and a half decades gone,
But, just seems like yesterday!

Funny, the Chess Game,
The Deity above does play!
That, he or she, the words here I do say!
Told, as a Tribute, to friends once seen__
A friendship, starting, seven decades ago!

π

Another Thought

The "ins", want to stay in,
And, the "outs", want to get in!
And others want neither to show!
But, then Nature, would quickly,
Fill the vacuum,
And, then only God or the Devil__
Would know, what we're in for!
"Ain't" politics great__ or not?

π

Then

It is hard to forget, those days,
When summer finally arrived,
And, school doors were closed,
And pad locked, besides!

And those early June days,
Just before "true" summer began!
Warm with time in the school- yard.

Running, playing and shooting marbles,
And the girls skipping rope,
And, the older guys (much bigger than I)
Escaping down to Gwynn's fall to skinny dip!

And me, left as the lone safety,
Patrolling the schoolyard__
And, trying to explain to my 6th grade teacher,
The advisor of the Safety Patrol,
Where Charlie Parks and George Hickman were!

I tried, but had no good explanation,
And, while Miss Wellner had me cornered,
The "guys" returned, and, caught: "wet headed"!
And their white safety cross-belts,
Were buried, in Miss W's desk drawer!

And then came the end of our years,
At P.S. 68, Betsy Ross Elementary School!

That was,
Almost three-quarters of a century ago!
And, I can remember,
So much and so many,
From a school no longer there!

Of, years and times,
And, people, and teachers to whom,
I never truly thanked
For being,
An important part of my life!

Maybe, just maybe,
If there is a life__ after,
I will get the chance,
To spend some time with them__ again!

Only, time, will tell.
And come a day__
My memories will be lost,
Except for the few
Versed in my books, if they still exist!

π

Let Not Books Disappear

There is a purpose for books in ink,
Or if you rather, a reason distinct!
For if writing is on a disc, a tape,
To play on an electronic device__
And no batteries or electricity be found,
A real piece of literature__ a book,
Has been known for centuries to exist,
And be available, as a "gift."

For it can be read, by the light__
Of the sun, moon, candles or a fire!
Or under the covers, with flashlight__
Like you did, when Mom yelled, "Light's Out."

And, thumb marked books on a shelf__
Make a den, a place to like

Sky Thoughts

Believe in "God" or not__
Humankind has always felt the need,
Of a deity, as his or her mentor to be!

From animals to the sun,
Then to many, Gods__ not just one!
Asians, then, added a flavor of their own!
And, in time, some Semites__
Elevated one, God alone!

And, then some, added to it__
With the Son of God!
Then to all__ human touches applied!

But here, billions, on this "orb in the sky,"
With unnumbered religions they try!
Many, mix Science and Religion__
And, at times, argue, fight and die!

I see Earth, as an "Eden" in its way,
Yet, we miss the opportunity,
Outlined in two words: "Golden Rule"
Which all, if in its clarity, believed,
No other rules, would humankind, need!

It's stupidity, avarice, jealousy,
And hate, that cause the failure to see__
That no matter what race, color, or creed__
We; every one of humankind,
Are Brothers and Sisters,
Beneath the skin, no matter what color it be!

Yet, no one truly knows, the real reason,
Why, in places__ different skin color was applied!

Unfortunately, I think humankind,
Will take, a long, long time, to fully accept,
That, all are brothers and sisters,
No matter what tint is applied!

And what a shame,
How great this belief would be!
That all peoples one day,
Would live in a world, of no color to see!

"Do unto others,
As you would have them do, unto you!"
So much truth in so few words!

π

The Unknown

His name, I never caught__
And he, never it volunteered!
So, John Doe we called him__
Till the day he disappeared!

And, when he was gone,
We mourned the "unknown,"
And, felt badly,
That "What's-His-Name"
Had not made us privy__
And, shared his moniker, with us to claim!

But, thought, maybe someday,
We might find out his name,
When we were grown!
But that was many years ago!

And, "Doe" to us, is still unknown!
π

Awake, am I

Was on a morn dark and dreary,
That my psyche raised a query,
A question about the sanity I possessed,
As, in the dark, I got dressed

Which put me to guessing,
And I thought maybe confessing
To things never done!
Would clear up any inconsistency!
But then I looked in the mirror,
Nothing there, was any clearer__
Except some wrinkles and hair grayer!
That, before, never bothered me!

But a feeling I had,
Of something, quite eerie,
Foreboding and imploding,
Something wrong, and goading!

Then my "bride" came into the room,
And the light turned on,
And, faced me squarely!
And looked at me quite strangely!
And, with venom in her voice
She said to me__
"Why are you, wearing,
My__ dungarees?"

So when I looked down__
Never again__ I vowed,
To dress, in a darkened chamber!
Nor ever, state, a diet for her__ might be a favor!

π

Changing Changes

This I am sure, that many find,
As the years "blow' by,
Your, mind goes back to days long gone,
And you see, vistas once known!

But should you, go to return__
You most likely find,
So much has changed,
You, begin to doubt your mind__
And, wonder, whether sanity,
Has gone, along with the time,

Or, a different place, you have found!
Now dropped, in your "recall."
And, you are lost and befuddled!
As if, a world, once known, never there at all!

This because, from the last time there,
Changes began taking place,
Never stopping__ and much to you, erased!
And, with each day, a difference made__
So much so__ little looked the same!
And yet, many, the same claimed!

And, you there, with, only bits to recall!
And all seemed wrong,
But for others, all was right,
But somehow, different as day and night!

No matter the age,
All must remain alert,
For change likes nothing better,
Than differences, with a brain to flirt!
And, change won't stop__
Unless, humankind__ this Earth deserts!

Yes, each generation,
Has a pension for change!
For change is new,
And, fresh for the young, to skirt!

And the young,
Sit not still, and have a will,
To make changes,
For the old, their minds to desert!

And then__ the next new "young"
Make the old young__ obsolete!
Ah, "change," sometimes, tis best to retreat.

π

Looking Back

Smoke from the campfire was rising__
In the near still air,
The moon cresting blood red,
A slight breeze,
Putting tree leaves astir__
In the oppressive summer air!
And, we, lost in the night!

The answer, to skinny dip,
On that night, so long, long ago__
That time now, seemed, as yesterday,
As the two of us chatted__
About, friends and days, once known.

They are, all gone now, and only us __
Those memories still to know!

A valued keepsake__ till the last breath to go!
π

A Friend and I

We, were talking
Just a few days ago,
Of days, before the days__
When old, we were!
And now those days, were long ago__
Before, old we felt we were!
And now__ truly old we are__
And hopefully,
Older yet will be__
And, here as long as we are__
For how long, as that long will be,
Is truly not, for "we" to know!

"Ain't" age, a funny thing__
When really young__
You wish to be older,
And then, at different stages of life,
Would like to swap ages,
Just, for a time, to be, or see!

For there is always,
A desirable age, that fits__
The moment, you want then!
Well, one thing that is sure,
Someday, you will age, no more!
So, make each day, and the age attained,
Be the best age, on that day, it can be!
And, on the morrow,
Do the same once again, and again!

Is there truly, one, best age__ to be?
Maybe if you are still alive__
Tomorrow__ is the one to be!

π

Reflective Moment

Have you ever, taken the time_
To realize, how many times,
You intended a thing to do__

And, allowed "whatever,"
To dissuade you, from your doing__
To, get things done?

Oh, if only, you did,
What you wanted, or should have,
Or, were tasked to get done
How better a person,
You might have become!

Oh, pity you! You slacker you!
That's, not a name, you want applied__
It will sully, your reputation for sure!

And, all you need to do,
To keep that name__
From being attached to you,
Is just to do,
What you know you should do!

However, by doing what needs to be done,
You will become a better "one!"
So get off of your butt,
And, get those and all things done!
And then the name:
Lazy, shirker, no-account bum,
Will never be attached to you!

Oh, your father, told me to send this to you!

π

Fuzzy Family Member
Rusty Tales!

Small, he was, the runt of the litter,
I think not as high as the coffee table,
But, big oh so big in his own way!
And, smart as a whip, from his first day!

I thought of our dog,
The other day!
After something came,
That brought a memory back!
What it was now, I can't recall!

He stayed for nearly 18 years,
And it still seems like yesterday,
That to doggy heaven was on his way!
Then I started juggling figures around,
And, thought, by gosh__ over two decades,
Have zipped away!

And to me, it is like,
Rusty, is still alive today!
So many great memories of him,
Come back, like they__
Just happened today.

When a pup__ well first his lineage__
Mother a toy poodle,
And daddy: part beagle,
And part toy collie!
The owners of the toy poodle,
Were not elated to say the least__
So, he to us, and then his brother,
To my mother-in-law,
Were, gifts, and be-gone, please!

Ours white, long brown ears,
And brown on the butt!
Oh, and long hair not fur!
And matted, first trip to the groomer!

It came off, like a pelt,
And, the brown never returned!
And, he never lost the love,
Of wife, husband and youngest son,
But, the older child__ shied away!

Not, that, Rusty didn't try,
But, it worked out okay—

With us, and his buddy the cat,
Across the street,
And son Paul's buddy Billy—
Next door, life was good!

He truly was a prince,
Among the canine species!
And, we never got another__
For, that dog__ set the bar too high!

Reviewing stories about the dog__
Trying, to control laughter and tears.
Is, a challenge, for certain__
I started listing Rusty Stories!
And laughter hurt my belly,
And, I could not stop smiling!

Just a few, would fill the space__
But each, led to ten more
For all, would need a whole book!
So, have selected, just one,
To capture and tell!

In our contemporary home,
In Western New York,
In the step down family room,
My wife had her dads, chair__
Actually, in the evening time,
Rusty shared his chair__ with her!

Curled behind her bent legs,
He spent the evening hours,
Until the news theme music,
Indicated, time to jump down,
And whisper (he did whisper),
To me, time to go out before bed!

There was this one night,
And take this in the right way,
That, dog, cut the worse "wind breaker."
Man has ever smelled!
He jumped, from the chair,
And turned and gave my wife a look,
No, one would believe
Giving blame, to the lady of the house!

My wife was quick to fan the air,
And very vocally denied ownership!
And, gave the canine full credit.
Rusty would have no part of it.
Came over to the couch where I was sitting,
And, actually sniffed the area,
Looked up at me,
And then glanced over to her.
And, jumped up on the sofa with me!

And, of course, I made a "smart-ass" remark,
Which went over like a lead balloon!
My "Bride" got up,
And went into the kitchen!

I guess I shouldn't have,
Called her stinky pants!
Rusty seemed to appreciate it
Gave me a doggy kiss,
And settled down, till the news ended!

All was forgiven by the next evening,
But, I paid dearly,
For the stinky pants remark!
And, we told the story many times!

I still see Rusty,
His red scarf around his neck,
Waiting on the landing
For every homecoming!
Just like it was yesterday!

You know, someday soon,
Those Rusty stories, I've got to do!
For both "She" and he, are now long gone!
And in honesty, I shouldn't be far behind!

And, it's only me, to write them down,
And, I want to tell you,
They are worth the time to read,
Probably a good book if done!
For that piece of fluff,
Was truly, one son-of-a-gun!

π

Satisfaction! It's, a pity, life has to end,
Just when, it seems, we humans are most comfortable
With life's answers to defend! Learning and Growing,
Is everyone's job in life!
Just ask "God" for Conformation!
π

A Look Behind

We were on George's Alberg 26,
Bow pointed down the Niagara River,
Passing the stone ramparts,
Of old Fort Niagara,
A jewel to visit!

And, as we entered Lake, Ontario
And, glided down the river
I looked down into its depths.
Flowing beneath our keel,

And was taken by surprise,
To see the bottom, as we glided by,
Clear was the water, deep__
The first time in years to see!
And realization took hold,
And, grudgingly, had to give credit,
To the Zebra mussels,
Those nemeses__ of destruction!

For with all the damage,
Those millions of "little buggers" did,
To Lake Erie, they had__
Cleaned the waters into Ontario.

That was now two decades ago,
Of conditions today, I've no idea.
My point; however, many times__
Even with bad, comes some good!

Seek and maybe yea will find!
An angel's wings, above the devil, flying!

π

Clocked as a Villain

You see it on your TV__
You feel it in your bones?
I hope you do, and will give these words:
A chance, and a thought, to propose! .

Are you grateful for: the COVID 19 virus?
Yes, I know you open your door in fear,
And a chill you get with each tolling
Of, another death to hear!

BUT, on the other side of the ledger,
That, rascal Virus, is bringing back_
Civility to most of our country,
Common courtesy and sense,
To a majority of the people!
Help for the hurting,
By the less hurt!
And, most of the country,
Is slowly drawing together!

Realization is dawning,
If Nature so desires,
Humankind, Is just a child,
Sitting naked, in the middle,
Of moving traffic!
Without togetherness__
Sooner than later,
Humankind will be "dust!"
God's dream, then, becomes a bust!

Maybe, just maybe__
The, right message will get through!
Do you get it?

π

Birth of Generations

By the stone marker he stood,
This, the last visit,
And the loss, he felt,
No easier, than times before!

But, this time,
His bags packed and in the cart!
The tariff paid and commitment made!

It was time, past time__
To get to the boat
And be gone, from country,
Village and coast, where born!

And felt inside,
Never again to return,
How could this be?
So much was a part of him.

And, yet deep down knew,
Life here would never again be!
For a big ocean now would be between,
And soon be, in Philadelphia town!

The year 1672,
Where many of the family Kinsey,
Now will be!
In a wild, untamed land!

I wonder if those,
That trip took__
Did ever dream,
Nearing, four hundred years later,
The family name would still be?

And, how many other families felt the same__
Knowing or not, in the decades to come,
They to help build a new country,
And, a new type of Nation!
No, not the first to arrive__
But part of a future to claim!

This, my mother's, mothers clan__
Who sometime in their first 100 years,
2o+ branches of 50 plus, crossed into Maryland.
Reason, lost to time, but Ancestors__
Who shared their DNA with me!
How many today, a count, I know not!
We just part of the makeup,
Of America!
A family history, a project worthwhile!

π

The Shrinking Globe

Smaller is our world in this day and time,
Speed and design has made this so!
Communications are even faster,
Covering nearly the whole Earth
With androids, smart phones, & more!

I am, not too sure, this is good,
But who am I, to make this claim?
Me, I would bring back the Pony Express__
If I could!
And slow down the fastest train,
Maybe then, "we" would have__
A saner world, once again!

π

Musical Mix

We cover our ears,
To the banging drums,
And, clanging symbols__
Of Life's disruptive corruptions!
And look to music,
To calm the "savage beast,"
That too often, bares its teeth,
And, chases us throughout life!

Seeking, always seeking__
Pleasant sounds to the ear.
And, music that differs,
Coming in varieties vast__
In human voices,
And with instrument choices,
And, venues, changing fast,
Throughout seasons, of the year,

Music is truly.
A language international
Notes can be read,
Regardless, of speech__ daily said,
Of people, wherever bred!
Music an art, a science,
Math based, fulfilling,
Talents, many and more than willing!

It travels the world,
Flowing like a stream,
Instruments, adapted and adopted,
Made with reeds and strings,
And, skins, on drums,
Metals and wood, by those that could!
And in churches and cathedrals
Pipes that to the ceiling climb!

And others are tootled,
And harmonicas in pockets reside,
And Bass Fiddles in a case do ride!
Pianos and organs with keys,
That, unlock sounds to please,
And so many others,
Hither and yon, that someday,
One day, be everywhere seen!

And let's not forget the voices,
In Quartets and choruses,
And solo concerts, and ensembles'__
Plus symphonies, of size,
Marching bands, bringing streets alive!
DJ's with discs,
And feet: to tap, clog and dance!
And other things, yet to add to the list!

And thank God for those,
Whose, careers are writing notes,
And, bringing new tunes to light!
And teachers who delight__
Bringing great talent into sight
And those electronic engineers,
Who like Bowes,
Gives us great sound in offices and homes!

Music, how would the world survive__
For any length of time,
Without voicing a lyrical verse __
Or playing notes of a kind,
Easing the tensions of the daily grind!
What a sad place,
Without music__ humankind would find!
Music, truly a gift of God!

Angels with harps,
A promise if to heaven one goes,
Even the devil has steam pipes to bang,
To lessen "hells" load!
For music can soothe,
Even that savage beast,
Is what, that saying does suppose!

Ah, music_ truly one of the wonders,
Of being alive!

π

Canvas on the Bay

Looking back a year or twenty,
Oh lets be honest_
Pushing more like fifty,
When, my body felt right nifty!
And that half-century mark,
Was to me, a good bit away!
I decided with a sailboat,
Was the big boy toy, for me to play!

So I put the "Grumman"
That had served me well,
On rivers and bays, for many days_
And, that had helped keep my sanity,
In those busy_ earning a living days,
In the back yard for a time to stay_
And bought my first "big boat"
A 26-foot, 1968 O'Day!

The year was near the mid-1970s,
An interesting time in our country,
Where, for $5000_ not a small sum,
For a Boy Scout Executive,

I got, a boat, I loved more than some!
That sailed on and near Chesapeake Bay,
But had to sell, when transferred far away!

My friend, Dutch and I, and others too,
Packed a lot of adventures,
In those years_ but oh, too few,
And upgrades, he and I made,
In cabin and cockpit in wintertime
With electric heater, polka music loud,
And "cannibal- sandwiches"
And, "she" was fast, and we were proud!

My family and I transferred.
A tough winter that was, in '77
The boat, moved, to the yard,
A submersible pump not enough,
To keep the water from freezing hard!

But, Dutch and I had one last sail,
Come spring, on the Chessie, that year,
Delivering the boat to an owner, new!
With me, choking back tears!

Friends we stayed, but unfortunately,
That, our very last sail_ for distance,
And 20 years, till another boat was mine!
However, those memories of the O'Day,
Are as fresh now, as when made.

Dutch is now gone_
But, not and never forgotten in my mind!
Nor is that boat, Aquila, "the Eagle"_
Flying a 180% Jennie, and we, all smiles!

π

Recognition

The gifts,
With which God blesses us,
Are many and great for sure!
But, who, is to say
Which is the more important?
Who is to state,
Which, we are to value more?

For, it is up to each__
His or her choice to make,
If a choosing were to be required,
To select the one,
That would serve them best!
And in honesty, for it to endure!

But, one could safely wager__
One gift, that would not,
Be allowed to leave the nest!
A prize among all and above most,
Each, and every moment in time!
Is, that thing, called: *"memory"*,
"A jewel of beauty", throughout life!

For it is here,
We capture every moment,
Each, scene that we espy!
Each feeling,
We have of friend & loved one!
And, billions of scenes,
Seen, by you and I.

Think of how many entries__
You carry__ for instant recall!
Think of your history available,
From, birth to last breath of it all.

Waste, few minutes of life__ use it all.
Yes memories are "gems"__
There, value, none can deny!
You, are privileged to gather them'
And, urged to enjoy them all__
Tis a plus, for the golden years,
When activities begin to stall!

Much thought has gone into,
Life, and time of living__
Each breath that is allowed
Is, a "Gift," to wisely, use__
For waste, brings from God __ a frown!

May you use wisely all gifts bestowed!
Large, small, quiet or loud!

π

Time in Place

When young, many times, wish to be older,
And, when older, oh, to be young again!
The former, comes with time,
And the latter, is never arranged!

So, live and live well,
In the time, at the time__ you dwell,
And, save the wishing,
For a "Wishing Well."

The odds are better on the first,
For, "doing" always wins the purse!

π

Truth, Fiction and Fact

Thinking lately, I have__
About the timing of one's birth,
And how history__ already underway_
Projects the outcome, of the unknowing!

Let me clarify!
I'm talking about birth in general,
And when born, decades of change,
Are already underway.

And the little one, __
Has little choice but to live it,
And, even less chance to affect it!
Till, twenty years are lost to time!

So that, day, of birth, dictates,
Much of one's march into history,
The, when, where, how, and even,
The, gasps of breath, to take!

For instance: my father's oldest brother,
Born just before 1900,
Drafted in 1917, in World War I
Was killed, and spent little time,
With his new born, 1916 son!

My dad, born in 1904,
Was too young for WW I, and too old for WW II.
Me, born in 1934,
Was, young, for, WW II, and Korea,
And, out of the service, before, Viet Nam!

So for dad and me, a different war did see!

Just, look at history through the ages__
And, many of the events never predicted,
Persons to be born had no control over,
Many by freak accidents became rich,
Many others worked their fingers to the bone,
And lived in poverty! And the rest, are others!

An interesting conundrum
Along, with a multitude of challenges,
Provided each day of life!
Perhaps, you should give history
The opportunity to tell you,
About your birth,
And, the generation, with little say, and the now!
- - - - -
Once upon a day dawning,
A child entered this world,
That he or she__ never asked to abide!

And, it is here, on an orb in the sky,
Must face the challenges,
Of breathing, life, and living,
Before, being, permitted to die!

And even then not a complete choice,
In the after life, where to reside!
And, many will tell you, a rough ride!

But just think, after the first two decades,
Tis your opportunity, to put
A thorn in history's side!

Not bad, for one
Who never asked, to be here!
And, now gets a chance,
On some things to decide!

π

Beyond

No one, knows,
When the door will close,
And a person known,
Is there no more!

And while one is gone,
Others, do live on__
Making life, the best, to endure!

All one can do,
Is live well, till time,
And breath,
Is gifted, no more!

How great it is,
To, copy the good,
From the "one" now beyond__
Left for all, for free!

And what you find new__
Tis a gift for you,
From a "being," no longer seen.

Then, place your, footprints__
On, your pathway in life,
As steppingstones gifted, by you,
To help all, in each day humans arise!

Let not the good memories go,
Of those, now gone,
For, they are, part of our lives!

In spirit and fact, at times
Somewhat, a mentor, in tow!
To draw upon,
When needed, as challenges grow!

π

Reminders

It was mid-January
It was raw, temperature low thirties,
And snow was in the air,
Clouds low, gray cover everywhere.
Oh well, its wintertime,
Just weather, one has to bear__
And, snow, no stranger here!

We in winter, and Australia
A hot summer, little or no rain,
And fire in the trees everywhere!
Other places heavy rains, and flooding!

Mother Nature, unhappy,
Has, her minions, causing chaos,
Of, all types__ everywhere!

It is more than, past the time,
For humankind, to pay attention,
To Natures' pangs__
If not, why not,
For, "mother" is taking the world to task!
Global warming, and, Climate Change__
Its here, you better believe, it's a fact!

So what, are we to do__
About this__ "mostly",
Self-made humankind situation?

Can there be, a worldwide,
Effort, to pay the price__
To, make the Earth safe again?
Or, is it into oblivion__ we slide?
Don't take too much time, to decide!

π

Born to Be

(A different time, my kind of place!)

The fighting is almost over,
Bullets flying, too many, too close,
I dropped my first rustler,
My first man, shot dead!
The sun is going down,
Soon darkness, yet much to be done!

My belly is growling,
My body is tired,
A blanket would be a comfort,
Maybe, in another few hours__
Yet, to put my head down!

No relief in sight,
Only the five of us are here,
We stopped the stampede,
Ran them in circle, till they bunched
Thank God, good water here!

I see on the horizon,
Against the setting sun,
Our cowboys coming back,
And, it looks like some rustlers
Tied up on horses, on leads__
The rest must be dead,
Damn, there will be hangings tonight!

Things are settling down now!
Cookie, just rang the chow bell,
But we will have to watch the herd,
Till the rest get coffee and are fed!
Right now, I'd settle for a biscuit__
And a place, to lay my head!

The watch is here, to spell us,
Boss, said chow down and catch some sleep!
We'll be back on night watch,
When midnight is on the creep!
There are three Rustlers,
Hanging from the cottonwoods!
They, no longer, a destiny to keep!

Yes, I think about those rustlers,
Damn fools,
Thinking that was an easy life,
A bullet or a rope__ is their prize!
If it hadn't been this time
Would have been sometime,
In, this year of 1888

My horse is now hobbled,
Munching' grass in a corral.
I put down, two full plates__
Of beans and bacon!
And a, big slice, of apple pie!
The run-in__ sure hasn't cut my appetite!

I walked about ten steps,
And, using my saddle for a pillow,
Wrote a few lines, in my book,
Rolled up in my blanket, and near died
But, I'll be ready, for night watch,
For, this cowboy life, will be mine__

One of the guys, is strumming___

- - - - -

And, when I die__
"Oh, bury me not,
On that lone prairie!
Carry me to__ the mountain high,
Where the trees do grow!

And, the wind, does blow!
And I can see, the land below!
And the moon and stars at night,
And the sun when it rises,
To give the morning light!
This best of all worlds,
For a cowpoke, like me!

- - - -

They brought his body home!
J. D. (Rusty) Broward 1871--1898
Sergeant, First U.S. Calvary,
"The rough Riders" Cuba-- July 1898
A great cowman, and even better man__
Too young, to be cheated, of a new century,
With, so many years yet to go!
Adios old friend!
Your notebook, I received, I'll read it someday!
Wyatt T.J. Everson, Rancher!

π

Verse, the Best of Vices

It is rhyme and rhythm
The lyrics of song!
Each if done well,
Its own masterpiece
Short or long, or in between!
It should sing as you read it,
And, return with its tune,
Each time to be read!
Yes, verse when you write it,
Writes well, with a melody in mind
And makes music of a kind
And comes back to you in time!
Even if musical notes, none can find!

π

To Be Found

Hear me good reader__
As I share a thought with you!
We (you and I) for one reason,
Or another, miss, much in life__

Which is our right to "grab."
By, taking advantage, of opportunities!
And capturing the simple beauty__
And, benefits, of the American dream!

If, you will invest,
Your time and diligence,
You will find a treasure trove,
Worth the effort you undertake,
And, a better life __ will make!

But, nothing is for nothing,
You receive, in proportion,
Of, the effort invested,
And good also shared__
As you travel through life!

Share not, and find,
The gain you get or got,
Seems to be less sweet,
With less meaning, in time!

Ready yourself, for opportunities to come,
And sharing; opening new doors,
And the return__ may be more than a lot!
Remember living the Golden Rule__
Is the best investment, one can get!
"Words, to pin your hopes on!"

π

A Message

Allow me! Allow me if you will__
To borrow your ears,
And instill__
A thought or two, into your mind!

Thoughts about humankind,
And, the trillions of their bones,
Once, skin covered and vitally alive,
With systems working,
And brains gaining knowledge__
With, every breath did survive!

This question, I pose,
To you this moment in time:

What, would be, your guess,
Since the beginning, of humankind,
How many, humans,
Have, left, a set of bones__
On, in or under land or water,
On this Planet__ where we reside?

How many zeros,
Would have to accompany__
That, first digit, in your surmise
Quad-drill ions, most likely__
And, even those, not a good guess!

And, with so much "Brain Power"
Available, through the ages,
Why, do we entertain, the stupidity of War__
And not live, in brotherhood for all?

How can we today,
Not see, skin is just a covering,
And under it, alike are we
With bones and parts there be!
With intellect, that can travel space,
And yet not heed Nature's plan.
And risk the loss of this Earthy land?

Why, do we have "good" and "bad"?
When with good, all can share,
A better world in every land!
There need not be Global Warming,
And with common sense,
Climate Change may not,
Be what now has begun!

Why can't all, adhere,
To, the Golden Rule,
And then no other rules__
Would peoples of Earth require?

Yes, death would still be,
A part of life,
Because all things have a time!
Nature shows us that,
And Nature has been here,
Millions of years before humankind!

For some reason,
An Entity with patience
Of a God, allows us to live!
How much longer, perhaps unknown!
But, humbly I say,
How much longer can the World,
Go on this way?

Tis not that humankind has not__
Had "**Warnings**!"

I know not the answer: BUT:
Perhaps: "*Do unto others*"
As you would have them do unto you!
Is simple and forth right,
As the answer gets!

"IT" gets my vote!
How about yours?

π

Tears Will Fall

If tomorrow, never comes__
Who will know it?
If it is COVID 19 that takes all away,
Maybe house pets__ will greave!
When someone's dinner, they become?

But if it is even more dire,
And animals and birds,
Go like the dinosaurs did!
Who or what will be left,
But, insects to keep score,

And, if they should go too__
That leaves just viruses and germs,
And, then who will be the winner__
For that will be unknown!
But, it sure won't be__ me, or you!

π

Words of Wisdom

Once upon a new day found,
With a sky of blue, and, birds singing loud,
I had reason,
To, help a neighbor lad,
And shared with him
Some words recently heard!

And, I remembered a ditty,
A Catholic friend of mind did say__
His Priest told him the other day__
"Never kick the Altar Boy,
For some day, Pope, he might be!"

Funny this "parable' at this time,
Came to me,
For to do that, never would I dream,
I worked with kids most every day
I saw the possibilities there at play!

But there is much wisdom,
In those words of rhyme,
And if all would those transcribe,
To fit life of every day,
A better world, be, worth the stay!

So listen neighbor, I said to him,
As through life you go__
Take heed of the sentiment,
In those words inscribed!

And, become a better person,
For all to know!

π

The Facets of Artistry

Like a diamond from the rough__
Found, cleaned and cut,
With untold facets,
Collecting light__

Art, is the history of life
In paint and pencil, clay, stone,
And metal fine,

And shells from beneath the waters,
Bits of cloth, woven in time
And, tapestries, on walls supplied!

Chalk on avenues in towns,
And spray paint on city walls!
Faces, sculpted on mountainsides!
Floors of mosaics, things you can name!
It's the stories of lucky people,
Granted a talent, during a lifetime!

Some can do a stitch in time,
Others a portrait or painting,
That for centuries can be prized!

There are watercolors,
And charcoal on cave walls,
That, for thousands of years survives!

There is sand into glass,
Heated, colored and blown,
That is displayed with pride!

There is clay, spun and urged,
By hand into pots, bowls,
Or, into forms divine!

There are buildings world wide,
Classical, modern, and others subscribed,
That are seen my millions of eyes!
And designs using wood,
In hundreds of different ways!
Barns, a favorite, of mine!

Castles and sculptures, of sand__
On beaches, some near fantastic,
There till the tide, bids them goodbye!

Chalk masterpieces on avenues,
That the rain steals away!
Or bracelets that glitter,
And, necklaces, that shine!

Or the beauty found in farm fields,
Of diverse patterns and colors,
Nurtured by seeds till the harvest yields!

And Nature; let's not forget Nature,
That the Master Painter
Creates, in outstanding ways!
Like, colors of leaves on a fall day.

And how about the quilter,
Who with skill, stiches and sews,
Bits and pieces of cloth
And makes, beauty for display!

And like a child, whose art
Is sacred, to a grandparent like me?
It is the prize, the beholder does see!

Yes, art is, the world,
With no limit of material used,
Or texture or how applied,

A piece of "Art" for one or all!
It be, singular or together find!
Each is an entity unto itself
Talent brings it alive__
The eye, and mind, of the viewer,
Become judge and jury__ to define!

π

Appalachian Recall

I was sitting watching the TV,
And, something triggered a thought,
And, on a pad nearby, I started to scratch!
And the years peeled away,
To the teen years and early twenties!

I remember those long weekends,
In September and through the fall,
The trail in Western Maryland,
Seemed waiting and ready for our call!

Mostly in Maryland we would trail,
But at times into Pennsylvania,
Or Virginia we found our way!

Up and up we would go,
Stopping at an overlook,
To see, the valley and land below!
The rainbow of colors, on trees in fall,
Fantastic, in their reds, gold's,
Crimsons, and millions of evergreen kinds!

In my day, the packs were not fancy,
Boy Scout type, or army surplus__
Horse-shoed of half a pup-tent,
Each Scout carried, on the outside!

Cook kits individual nestled,
Food, most times scrounged at home,
Canteen and ax on hips, hanging low!

A night under the stars,
And at times in rain or snow!
And campfire, songs sung,
With voices changing, as age was won!

There were always, trips and places,
To learn Scout Craft and have fun,
And, Merit Badges and Rank advancements
And, from adult leaders, life lessons spun!

And we, stayed, till scout days were done!
And, I remember those times__
Truly, they were much more, than just fun!

And even some of the older "guys,"
Who, were there, then__
Whatever happened to them?

But the times in the mountains,
And that sky full of stars,
And the learning to work together!
Has stayed with me__ these years!

And, our leaders, men who truly cared,
I doubt we ever fully thanked them,
Maybe soon__ in person will finally do!

Yes, these are an old man's memories,
Of times, I so wish, the kids today__
Could capture and store away!
Too bad, those days didn't stay!

π

Twist of Fate

Across the state line,
On the highway drove,
Turned on, old route 459!
And in time, into the hills
Climbing up all the while,
To the foot of the mountain,
Where serenity, could find,
My road, once a trail; years ago
That, the "red man" knew well,
Where lightening had struck the giant Oak
That tree, centuries, old__
Still standing, still alive,
And, a sentinel waiting to greet me__
As I arrived! I felt, near home!

I pulled in far enough__
To open the log gate,
And then in further, to pull it closed.
And, drove and drove,
Up the rough mountain road!
Slowly, so slowly,
Missing, low spots and high.
Till I reached that cabin,
Nestled in pine and hardwoods,
As it had__ for those many years,
Been, it's history supplied!

I pulled up to the cabin,
To unload food stuffs and gear
But first walked to the lake
To see if the beaver were still there,
And then out to the overlook,
To see the valley far below!
And breathe in, fresh mountain air!

Unlocked the cabin,
And put stuff away,
Rolled up my sleeves,
And, put a broom into play!
It took a while, to ship shape the place,
Opened the windows, to air out the space!
And again as always, "marveled"
At the workmanship, the man created!
And then with ladder in place,
Up to the chimney with tools in hand,
Cleaned the flue, neglected for a span.
Then with the chain saw,
Cut to size a half a cord or more,
Of logs I had piled a while before! __
And split and stacked them,
On porch and on the cabin floor!

With a sandwich in hand,
And feeling just fine,
I walked with my camera
On this land I now called mine,
Photos I took of things to be done,
And, the beauty to be seen,
So much beauty, to the eye now won!
There is a story of this cabin,
And the mountain and land,
But, since darkness is coming,
A fire in the fireplace I set,
And, the oil lamps, I readied to light.
And, lit off the old iron stove!
Dinner, fried steak and potatoes,
And, a beer or three!

I settled down by the fireplace,
To ruminate, for a time to take,
Some years ago, when about 18,
I took a bus to spend a week,

In the area up in this direction!
Pack on back, hitching when I could!
Well, long story short,
Two guys, were giving an older
Black man, a real hard time.
Stupid or not, I dropped my pack,
And jumped in, to help, the old man.
The two oafs started to lose,
And, one pulled a gun,
And, I put him, down hard.
And, then I had the gun!

They couldn't get to their truck,
I, was in the way, I waved the gun,
And, sent them running down the road,
And, then fired, a shot, into the air.
The old man was hurt a little,
But, was up on his feet
"Get your gear and get in my truck!
"We need to get out of here," he said!
"In a minute" I said,
I put a bullet their tire,
That, I thought should be a lesson learned__
He laughed and off we went.
"Thanks " he said, Not as young as I used to be!"
"You did okay", said I
And, then we introduced ourselves!

The upshot, was,
I spent my first night at that cabin,
And, many other nights,
In the years to come__
When home from college,
And on leave, from the military!
He taught me wood working,
And, a million other things,
He, became, a grandfather I never had!

I had about finished my tour overseas,
My folks got in touch with me,
To tell me, Oz, had died.
I felt a sadness, a hurt,
I never felt before!

It wasn't long and I was home!
My days in the military done__
And, on the porch, was the latest__
Off-spring of dogs, he had raised,
And, it was like, that pup, knew me,
And the tears flowed!

There was also, the deed,
For the cabin and mountain land!
The only caveat, "do it proud."
And, know you will!

Next weekend, the dog and I,
Will introduce, "the Land near the sky"
To the girl to be, that new wife of mine,
And, from photos she has seen,
Is, already smitten,
And, a new chapter will begin!

And, Oz's photo is on the cabin wall,
One I snapped long ago.
It's too bad, he and my she,
Never got each other to know.
Hopefully, we will have kids,
Who on the mountain will grow!

I pray, Oz, will like the legacy, I grow!

π

A Chair Once Ours

And there we sit in a high chair,
Just a tad, in those moments then,
And the years begin to tumble,
And change and new days do descend!

And soon through the decades,
We slip and slide,
And it's not us, in the mirror,
It's another face that abides!

What happened to the us we knew,
In those days now gone by,
Where is that youth,
We boasted with pride!

And the years keep going,
And, it gets harder to keep up,
And keep flab at bay,
And, seems like more to do, every day!

And, who stole that youth,
While we were aging inside!
Changes, and always more changes,
Overwhelming, our given time!

The one, who, stole our youth, away,
Should be apprehended,
And duly convicted,
Of a, mortal crime, and have to pay!!

But, Just give me back my youth,
And, all will be forgiven,
If only those Halcion Days,
On the morrow, be captured alive!

π

Just Sitting

I sit in my easy chair,
Eyes cast down,
And, see visions of "old" friends,
Some, gone, others still around!

I see, most of them, as young__
Even those I still see today!
A few in old age,
But, find many of them
Now living, with little to say!

How great the world seemed,
Before, Father Time, knocked at our doors,
Bringing, grey hair and wrinkles,
And, aches and pains,
With each call, he records!

His, visits, are, just, a part of life__
And, some of his responsibility,
Is, *population control*!

But why, can't he accomplish__
What, needs to be done,
Like an "Angel of Mercy",
By, keeping, our exterior, young!
Not as a prune, over-dried!

Just a word to St. Peter,
To give, Father Time, a note,
Folks may not be against dying
If they knew, at the Pearly Gates,
A, good-looking corpse__
Is how they would come!

π

Another Gathering

It was a burned out house,
The lot vacant now,
And the old couple from next door,
With the help of friends,
Cleaned it up, with an idea to restore!
But, there they started planting,
In and on that urban lot,
That once was part of rural spot!

Fruit trees, not a full orchard, mind you,
And vegetables, flowers and bushes,
And each year it grew,
With the help of neighbors,
They produced a good harvest!
Shared with the neighborhood!
It became a place,
Where children came, to frolic and learn,
And a place of "green"
That many, in pride returned!

And in the fall, well before,
The first snow came,
The neighbors put together a picnic,
That was called *"The Gathering!"*
And, everyone knew
They, a part, now of a tribute__
To the, old couple, "lost to view"!

There was a lot of gray and wrinkles,
And, young tots, of families__
That recently moved in!
And, it was truly__
A *gathering*, of, many tasty things,
And, always, a Story Board to begin!
Now "two lots", at the end of a city block,

A place, that pride kept alive,
And fresh fruits and vegetables,
Were aplenty, in growing months!
This, told a story of people, faces and races
Who learned, how to be "one"__
Working together in a cultivated patch!
A harvest of people__ **In a Gathering Spot!**

π

Changes, Pages & Ages

So many things available today,
Were not in, the market__
When my dad was young!

But, if you could ask those then alive__
A good bet you could make__
Would be, they would say:
Oh, give me life, as it was back then!

Of course, they were young__
And the world was a different place!

But you know, I for one__
Would agree with them!
And, your memories if you will review,
And look at your yesteryears__
Most likely, that be, your choice too!

Much seemed better then,
Better than, what you now do face!
Except for electronics, medicines,
And, perhaps a few other things (?)!
But, forward is the name of the game!
And, is change; memories are pages of recall!

π

Playgrounds of my Youth

A city kid was I, in Baltimore town!
Near 7, at the Great Depression's end__
Then molded by the Second World War.

And, in honest truth,
Never knew we were poor__
Because I don't remember,
Ever missing a meal!
Unless__ I was sent to bed,
For misbehaving,
A misdemeanor, Mom said!

But to me life was good.
There was no TV in those days
There was school not far from our block,
And after, changing clothes,
It was out to play, until, suppertime,
And then homework!

There were no fancy recreation plots
Our playgrounds, were the allies,
And streets, and back lots!
And house walls for __
Pitching, baseball cards,
Or bouncing and catching tennis balls,
There was, no Little League,
We would choose up sides,
And, ruled our own games!

There were rubber band guns,
With ammo from, old inner tubes.
Wooden swords, for battles fought,
And marbles for shooting,
And old skates nailed to 2 x 4s,
That became, orange-crate Scooters!

And the back allies were,
Our domain,
If trash, garbage, and huckster trucks
Weren't rumbling up and down!
And, the Ice Man,
Where we got slivers to chew!
And back yards for Monopoly and such!

And after supper, Duck on the Rock,
Tin Can Jimmy,
Fire truck #9,
Tag, and Catch me if you can,
Red Rover, Red Rover
The list was truly endless!

There was Gwynn's Falls Park,
Or the "lot", or Ashton Street,
When snow was on the ground!
There was Blue and Yellow dams,
With ice skates, when Dad,
Would load up the car!
And keyed, roller skates,
On bumpy streets!

There were games and "stuff",
For each season of the year!
We might have been poor in dollars,
But we were rich,
In something to do, all of the time!
And, so many people, in their way__
Mentors looking out for you!

**Too bad, kids today,
Are richer, but poorer in so many ways!**

π

All Because

I entered the house,
As done a thousand times before,
The old man,
Now seated in his rocking chair!

Head down on his chest,
Deep in a sleep,
Far different from my entrance,
Those many years, coming in before!

He a grouchy bastard,
Me thinks__ from first breath at birth,
But damn good he was to me,
From first meeting, decades gone!

When at 10, our real first contact,
Me, trying to recover a ball
From his side of a high fence!
And, me halfway down the fence!

His first words "sic um dog!"
And his laughter, when I fell in the mud!
My first words: "Now I'm going,
To get a licking, my jeans are dirty!"

He laughed again, and said:
"Well, we can't let that happen, can we?
And that was the beginning,
Of a forty year friendship!

He had some relatives, but talked to none,
And, became like a grand-pappy to me,
Teaching me stuff, from A to Z.
And, now, time, nature and old age__
Was calling the play!

He woke with a start,
And saw me and smiled that smile of his,
And, grinning said:
"I signed my will yesterday!"

"What's the rush", said I?
"Oh, he said and smiled again.
"Cause, I wanted to be sure,
You got this here rocking chair!"

Then he laughed real hard,
"I still owe a few payments on it,
And, I knew you'd be the only one__
To make them"—and laughed again!

"Its sort of __ nest egg,
When you get old like me!"
"Get the bottle and lets share some!"
And we drank and talked!

He died that night,
And I cried a lot,
And his funeral just days away!
That for me, a truly sad, sad day!

Well, those relatives got nothing at all.
Me. I got the chair,
And, a copy of the will, which said,
It's all gone, not even a penny to share!

I made the last two payments, on the chair!
Could hear him laughing, loud!
Got an envelope from the lawyer,
Truly sealed, wax and all. I saw his smile!

It wasn't a long, letter, but mighty fine!

"I love you boy, and hope you feel the same!"
"You've been a pure blessing to me,
And made my miserable life have meaning, again!"

"My chair, is a great chair,
And, I hope for you, as it was for me__
If there is too much stuffing, fix it to suit!"
Be a great "nest egg" for you!
God Bless, keep those fishing reels oiled!"

After my memories and tears stopped,
I pulled the chair into the light,
And, sat on the stuffing high,
Uncomfortable as the devil, I found!

So I took the stuffing out.
And there, found a deed__
To those acres by the river,
Where we spent so much time!

And the tears ran again!
And, next a bankbook in my name
With ¾ of a million dollars!
Then, how comfortable that rocker became!

All happening because of a lost ball,
And a fall in the mud,
And so many wonderful years,
With and older friend!

I knew, what he wanted done,
No need to write it down,
We had "sky larked" many times__
"What if", never dreaming he had the money!

I'll get it done, & a lot of kids, will know my friend!

π

Knowledge, is Found

I climbed a mountain, one day,
Well above the line of trees,
A barren place on the top,
Just rock, the sky and me!

The vista from this very top,
As the sun, through high clouds__
Did appear__
Painted all, in pure beauty,
This to me, was payment received,
And, a memory obtained,
For, the effort and time,
I invested, for the vision to see!

I sat on a rock and turned
The Compass, three-quarter round,
And, was dazzled by,
The color and texture, of the scene!

Then suddenly a storm cloud appeared,
And engulfed me,
With, sleet, snow and rain,
Soaking and battering me__
But gone then, as quickly as it came,
Leaving me, cold and shivering!

But, with the sun came warmth,
And, a truth it gave to me:
"Life is good, but challenging,
Stand fast, and much you will learn _and_ see!"
Tis a simple truth, if you, will but believe!

π

Future Choice

I hope you will or would,
After perusing these words you find,
Agree with me__
The premise of my effort,
Is hopefully to open many
Eyes and minds!

Now tis only my thought,
For I have never heard
Any other to state this premise,
With clarity and insight__
And, I cannot but wonder, why not!

For when God or whatever deity__
Put humans upon this earth,
It is my opinion, he or she
Was looking for Caretakers,
To mind and look after,
The gifts, that deity, gave at birth!

And somehow, most of humankind,
Got mixed messages and ideas,
When, the instructions were given out__
And while some were kindled,
Most were lost early on__
But, tis time now, for their full rebirth!

Except__ for some, who see and do__
Some parts of the task to be done!
I have a great concern,
At how much is yet to do, in time,
To get and excite others,
To be the caretakers,
In the deity's plan as spun!

For there is no question,
That for millennia, humankind__
Has, abused, this planet Earth__
So if you want this earth for now,
And, for generations__ yet to come__
Each Earthly person, a "Caretaker" must be__
And follow Nature's marching drum!

Or__ prepare, to see,
This Planet's' "End of Days"__
Soon to come!
Be it, "On your Watch!"
One, would think, your name__
Be "MUD,"
If you, allow, this, disaster__ to come, to "Bud"!

But, if saved__ a heavenly reward,
May yet__ to you come!

π

Snake Eyes

When the dice are tossed,
And, the number is seen,
It could be your number__
Your, very last number!
Or it may not be!
But, chances are, someday__
The last toss, it, will be!
Life is a game.
And, the wise among us__
Play it, to win, as long as they can.
Are you wise__ or otherwise?

π

A Vision to See

I know not why, in time and place__
When breath is mine
And, few challenges face,
I walked the miles,
Once ran the race,
And still feel in life,
I must prove my case!

This makes no sense to me,
For, I have, served my country__
And, my community,
And, a family, have raised,
And taxes all paid,
And even today,
Help others on their way!

What now, at my age__
Is truly expected of me?
Perhaps, it is time for me,
To, sit, in a chair__ and watch TV?
Why now in my dotage years
Am I expected a load to tote?

And as I sat on the front stoop,
A child came up to me
And said: "mister, please tie my shoe"
And, I looked at her, in my rage,
And her smile stole my heart away!
And then I knew what I had to do,
For in that moment God spoke to me,

So, the very next day,
I signed up a "Santa" to play!
To be with "kids," memories to make,
And stories to tell!

And, when Christmas was done,
A grandpa to play,
To help families in need!
What better way,
For me to end my days!

There is a vision waiting for you,
Of things for others you can do,
Don't waste the time, left to you__
And what better way,
Than, to help, as many as you can!
That is your legacy, to carry through!

Just think what the world could be__
If all people, took Brotherhood seriously!

π

Hark, the Reasoning

To, "*gather*" is to understand,
That most things, matter more__
When you, put them in a proper space!

There is a challenge, all must face!
When you take__ it or them,
To, the "*Gathering Place.*"
For here, or there
Or any such site,
There are, things to accomplish
In all the days, of your life!

Whether it be business,
Or war, or writing, or just living_
Full success, depends on final disposition,
Of "everything" into the "right place!"

π

Time Warp

High school, done!
First year of college,
Thank God its summer time,
Bored out of my mind

A summer job in a Refinery,
This at the time was more than okay!
Sometimes, down on one of the docks,
Tying up barges, or crude carrying ships!
This was okay!

One thing, that stands out
In my memory_ are, the workboats
Coming from Curtis Creek,
Loaded with watermelons for Baltimore!

We would yell "hi" to the crew,
And they would wave back.
And toss a ripe melon into the water,
Then, we would pick it out,
As the wake pushed it in!

That melon, fresh picked,
We carried to the lab,
Put it on ice, for a lunchtime treat!
Those days in the'50s,
A good time to recall!

That summer job, turned into nine years,
Dropped college for then,
Two years drafted in the army,
Promoted a number of times,
And then left to finish,
College, and a career in the BSA!

You know,
No complaints can I, make,
It was a good life,
Blue in the collar,
And then white shirts and uniforms,
And hopefully, "doing good" every day

First in Baltimore, then to the Boston area,
Seven years, and four on, the Regional Staff__
More than half of Massachusetts,
And the whole of Vermont!
Then, to the Buffalo Area,
Till and little after retirement time!
Then home to Maryland!

This last decade plus,
On the Eastern Shore of Delaware
How fast time, slips away!
Truly, an old timer's lament!

I tell you this,
Because, I've had a great run,
So many and much I have done,
That, never thought I would do!
And, now, I continue to work__
My legacy __ books I write in verse,
Not done yet I hope, is true!

Why I share, this bit of it,
Hopefully to convince you,
A legacy to begin or continue,
I think you will find,
It will be enlightening
To your family, at the right time!
Not necessarily verse,
But a story perhaps, you too will write!

π

Country Ours

Who am I to say they cannot do,
But when their life is through,
What legacy, with thought imbued,
Can, anyone say: theirs is true!

Who are they, you ask of me?
Why they are the fools,
Who try to undo,
The fabric of a great land!

We now call them aliens,
Not from a planet far,
But from countries,
Where, unhappy they were!

And, brought their unhappiness,
To our shores,
And felt we should support them,
Even as their language, refuse to lose!

And they will not accept,
The ways in which,
Our ancestors, built a great country,
Where they wanted to abide!

We learned the very hard way,
Immigration is a hard game to play,
But, needs strict rules,
For those, who are welcomed in!

And, not all can make the grade,
And must be sent back,
From whence they came
Or in little time, they, be our shame!
Other thoughts are inane!

Think not, and bear the stain,
Just look at other lands,
This plan failed to provide.

Yes, tis a shame,
And does not seem fair,
But one hole, leads to more,
And the ship-of-state, is no more!

Freedom is not free,
It is an investment from all,
And, all must, subscribe___
To the plan___ of proven success!

This land we claim,
Learned from wrong, to make right,
And learns more each twenty-four
But must hold to the basic tenet.

Get me not wrong
We have been and are,
A nation of faces, from all places!
But interwoven into a fabric fine!

This accomplished not without,
Much passion and punching,
Which even today, remains,
The basics, of 250 years must be sustained!

How many millions, have proven
The plan, in play, must stay___
If the nation is to be!
The "new" must adapt___ or stay away!

Need I say more!

π

But Better Could Be

History, records actions done,
Facts, logged in script or mind,
For recall, hopefully as truth in time!
Large amounts, written in blood!

Even when known in human minds
Off times put aside,
Forgotten when passion boils!

And many times it explodes,
When a sociopath, speaks in tongues,
And claims a war can be won,
By sacrificing the young!

And goals of a despot to be,
Others' lives and fortunes,
Are just honey under the tree__
Till the despot is put down,
And, the next one History sees!

Historical "logs", a learning tool
But too soon forgotten,
Or hidden from view!
And if not seen and understood,
Repeated, for the good, of only a few!

But, would be a blessing true,
If humankind, would history use,
To make life for generations
A warless world, and peace to view!

Will you, be, one__ of the ones,
To, make this, for our country come true?

π

A Mountain Trail

It seems to me, this trail
Was not so high,
The last time I was here!

Of course it had been a long time,
And this most likely my last time,
Boot prints I would make,
And, just glad this day I could!

I look across the valley,
As, I had done, those years before,
There was still beauty seen,
But less I thought, in memory caught!
Too much, civilization, now there!

Too many, trees gone,
Replaced with buildings everywhere!
But one could still catch a whiff
Of Nature, in the air!

But not the same
And, that is a shame,
So much, too much,
Causing many, great despair!

Yes, I know, nothing__
Stops, change, from putting memories__
To a test__ to recall! But, some___
Would have declined, any change at all!

And, I feel the same way,
Of gray hair and wrinkles
And old skin that crinkles,
That Father Time leaves,
Now when he comes to call!

As I stood there at the overlook,
A family up the trail did arrive.
And they oohed and ahhed__
At the vision seen

And the father turned to me__
And said: "Wow, what a vista to see."
"Yes, in deed", I replied, smiling,
And turned, homeward bound!

Beauty is captured,
In the eye of the beholder,
At his or her, time in place,
And, it is like a snowflake,
No second time,
Will ever be the same, in that space!

If, you ever go back,
Be wise, and treat each visit, as a first__
And hold memories, each unto it's own,
And then, no conflict, takes place!

π

Waking Wisdom

Now I want to tell you a truth!
As I've gotten longer in the tooth__
I fully realize, with little surprise,
Many things, I didn't__ but wished, had tried!
When my memory was good,
I wish I had learned more!
And, when my back was fine,
More mountains, I wished I had climbed!

But, now, excuse me: it's my naptime!
π

Empirical

Some random thoughts I share,
Perhaps, as guidance if you care!
As an old, to a new friend to be!

Verse my friend,
Like the "lyrics" of song
Many times in your mind remains!
But, for many of us,
Music cannot write,
Or, notes read, or an instrument play__
It is for us, the scourge of life!
Me, I am one of those,
But__ I take heart: with verse__
That comes, to me, like lyrics stay!

First your name: of it, be proud,
Write boldly for tis a gift__
Passed from down the line!
From ancestors of thine!
Tis yours to have__ make it shine!
Learn something new each day,
Waste not your precious time__
Your brain will expand, with demand!

Do, good for all humankind,
And that, good will return to you!
Keep your body strong,
And, a fuller life__ will be thine!
Make life a game to play,
Honest, in all ways,
Share love along life's way!
And make Verse your Vice of living__
The words of songs, your melody of life!

π

Vision

Things now, I see,
Through a prism, different
One, not that I fully understand,
Nor, its colors wholly entertain!

Nor any longer,
Truly care to contest,
But, if not me, who will?
And, why should they?

There is truth to follow,
Which, many won't digest,
Unless taking the time,
To peruse, and confess,
"Guilty", is their attitude at best!

With this last generation or so,
The gap of understanding widens,
Until, it is a gulf, far, to the old!

What has, happened__
To: "He's not heavy,
He's my brother!"
To now, when everything__
"Is for me?"

In this year 2020,
I have a little hope,
Of, all people, adjusting, to COVID 19.
Or the like!
For, much, selfishness is in play!

Not having paychecks'
That economic impact
Can't, fully be understood!

But ignoring social distance,
And, "not" covering ones, nose and mouth,
To protect "others"__
From your virus, carried,
Is a senseless childish act!

And, to berate Governors,
For trying their citizens to save,
Is adolescent in every way!
And not worthy, of a National foray!

And, placing your butt in venues,
To rub more than shoulders,
Is truly depraved!

When, and it is when__
COVID 19, comes flying back,
Because of stupidity,
Much bigger numbers__ will apply.
Many more will die!
Tis too bad, other than, the guilty,
Will also die!

π

Truth: A Pill to Swallow

All words need an open mind,
In order to find, acceptance__
In a place, if they are to remain,
Sustain, survive, and have impact,
In the world, as fact!

To cast them aside when truth resides,
Is a loss, to all humankind!

π

When, the Sun Rises

I moved from the horizontal,
To the vertical upright, position,
For awake I seemed to be,
And headed to the bathroom__
Time for a shave, and new day to see!

Now__ who, is that,
In the mirror, looking back at me?
"Oh God, it's me!"
Where, is the younger me__?
That I knew and thought__
I would see, not this older me!
Looking as if, vitality, is fading away__
Could it be, the younger is hiding inside?

I pause, and a breath I take,
As thoughts of days now gone,
And, those times of "then",
When, places and of course, faces,
Once known, were freshly seen!

Those now, most likely__
Would never be met again.
Churn I do, sweet memories
Of days and years,
Laughter and tears,
And, the good life, known then__
Visit for a moment, again!

I pause for seconds more!
And wonder__
If, I ever truly said Thanks__
For all of my given days!
And, the breath, each day,
That was and is pretty great!

Perhaps, this is a reminder for you too?
Just a simple "Thanks"
Costs so little, and does so much!

Like: "Thank you God for each day granted,
And, help me, do good in time allotted,
And allow me to serve thee, as am able!" Amen!

Well, on with this new day, now begun!
Some mornings are educational
But, not what I now, would call fun!

π

Just Thinking Thoughts!

The gift of breathing air!
Doing, pretty well what you please!
Misusing Mother Nature's hospitality!
Until, the "Piper" wants to be paid__
From whence, does the payment come?

Tis just an assumption,
But, leads to a question__
How come, the world__
Is in such a screwed up condition?
Did you (humankind) put it in that position?

Yeah, I know, I just created,
Another challenge,
A conundrum, an enigma,
In a puzzle, and a question,
With an answer__ unknown!

Or, perhaps it's a timely discussion?
Before it's too late for change to overcome!

π

Life in Context

There was time, somewhat, long ago,
I gave a girl a kiss for show,
She slapped my face hard, quite a blow__
And said, I'm not that kind of girl you know,

Well, I knew she lied,
Cause, I'd seen her before,
Kissing boys on the gym floor!

Or in a doorway down the street,
Or other places,
Where boys and girls would meet.

How many boys, she kissed before,
I was told, many had scored,
So I began to think,
Kissing girls was not for me!

That, perhaps like a Priest,
A celibate I should be,
And, then there be, no slaps for me!

Then, I met Bonnie Sue,
And, kissing her was the thing to do!

And, then decided, being a Priest,
Was never going to be the thing for me,
And, I was Lutheran__ anyway!

So now the years have fled away,
Six damn kids in my yard do play!
And that wife of mine,
Says no more kissing, Hon!
Or hanging your pants on the bedpost, son!
Get yourself a hobby instead!

So now I'm back to where I was,
Those many years before!
But hurting more than the slaps I bore,
And, working two jobs,
To feed kids__ who just keep eating more!

To hell with life like this,
I thought one day,
After I heard a stranger say:

Go tell your wife,
This is how; it's going to be!
After, you get yourself a vasectomy!

Well, we get together once in a while,
And, we kiss a lot, and give a smile,
Just waiting for the kids be grown,
And move away!

And then, to chase her around the bed
Like, those games we used to play!
In those days that have fled away!

Just think it started,
With a hard slap on a teen-age day!

Now, watching my kids,
Those older ones I see__
The same damn games,
They are starting to play!

Oh hell, they'll figure out,
Somewhere, along life's way!

But, change it not__ no I say!

π

Fact, Fancy & Future

Look, the world, somehow,
Has always melted into__
A caste society!
With a top, middle and bottom!
And, when the top gets too extreme,
The bottom, takes to deadly action,
And the whole system dissolves!

And then the cycle begins again!
But, with the brainpower of humankind,
There surely is a way to find__
A means, and method,
To make humankind a "Brotherhood"__
The golden ring to find!

The way the world is today__
Cannot, be the plan__
That God, had in mind__
When he made Eden__
Of this Planet land!

Note, skin color is a "shade",
Where first humankind was placed!
Under the color__ inside humans, are the same!
Except, blood types, they differ,
But, cross color lines, matches made!
With that understood, shouldn't__
All other oddities, be easily decided?

And a better world obtained,
For each and everyone?
Should you think not__ why not I cry?

π

Perusal Potential

Pay attention to what I say!
"A good idea, you should not__ let, get away"
So here are the nouns and verbs
And other parts of speech,
For you to put to work!

All, should turn their hand to writing,
Of course not all Shakespeare will be,
How boring, that would be to see!
But each should pull good thoughts,
From ones' memory trove,
Ink them down, before they are gone
And, can't be found.

Then when embossed in ink,
Give them to kids, so they too can think!
And, perhaps someday a treasure become!
A legacy, for you, of your words,
More than dust, when you are done,
And, I mean, truly done!

Maybe, they not seem to be,
A great gift when given,
But when found tucked away for a time,
After a number of years,
Just might be a thing to find!
To remember you,
When all, are sipping a glass of wine!

And, you thought what I had to say,
Wasn't worth the time of day__
See how wrong you can be!
Ta, Ta

π

A Facet of Time

Green leaves, small and tender,
In early, April, is fodder, for, high-winds,
That, delight in sheading, tree limbs,
Turning them into a winter sight!

Trees, but following the pattern set down.
Now have to play a different game!
To refurbish, the bare limbs
While the sap is running, right!

Why does Mother Nature play this game?
When winds of March and the equinox,
Have passed weeks before?
And the softer rains of April,
Have turned grasses and else to green?

Is it mans' selfishness and stupidity,
That makes, Mother Nature sore?
That throws off her seasonal routine,
And brings her anger to the fore?

Can we as humankind, not see our crimes,
Across every, Earthly Land?
The Bible talks of "Eden'
But perhaps "Eden" is just a metaphor,
For our "Planet Earth",
A work, of incomparable worth!
And be treated, the way, it should be!

Unfortunately to say, tis time Earthly abusers,
Be dealt with__ before our Earth,
This gift of gifts: is taken away!
Speak out, if you know another way!

π

A Step Beyond

Few seek pain!
For pain is an anathema__
To most of humankind

And, yet I think of the many,
Who in pain, do pass,
And my thoughts turn__
To, ask why?

Humankind, knows not all things,
And, yet have walked on the moon,
But, have conquered not Pain__
And, I again ask why?

"Some" pain perhaps,
Is, a guide, in finding, a weakness__
And, this could bode well,
For reasons, in time!

But on the whole,
What other reason,
Is, there for pain?
And, why, should it not go?

Ah, a conundrum for you,
Perhaps to puzzle through,
Or even an enigma, to face,
For you, and the human race!

Or, maybe you will be the one,
Problems will solve__
And in history,
Your name will be placed!

π

I must confess

When a thought invades my space,
I know I must, react apace,
If not, loss of it, is assured,
And most times it returns not,
To my mind, ever more!

I wish this were not so,
Not that the thought wouldn't come__
But that when arriving,
It, would stay until, I dismiss it__
After, it is written & stored away!

Now, I have been blessed,
With a small talent found.
And for some reason,
Verse to me is amplified,

Verse, one of the best vices of man!
Many times, holds a place,
In ones mind__ like lyrics of a song!
That replays at times!

And for me, who can't,
An instrument play,
Or musical notes to read,
To be God's scribe, inking verse,
Is a gift, lovingly received!

And the best to you I can wish__
I hope and pray, you have a talent__
God has gifted to you,
And, while at times, an onus can be
You accept and employ for posterity!

π

CPSIA information can be obtained
at www.ICGtesting.com
Printed in the USA
BVHW080400250521
608002BV00007B/1674